Black meat and Black streets (urban shower tales)

ISBN:978-1-312-75129-3

By:Anthony Hawkins

Cover Art By Anthony Hawkins

Dedicated to the gay and lesbian community.

Warning:This book contains graphic explicit and mature content.

Tale # 1:His uncles homeboy

By:Anthony Hawkins

Cover Art By Anthony Hawkins

Dedicated to the gay and lesbian community.

Warning:This book contains graphic explicit and mature content.

Prologue

Jabar was a very handsome 23 year old very smooth chocolate brown colored skin young man with thick dark hair and a very sculpted and toned physique,and he also lived with his stern nonbiological uncle Vinny,both of them sharing rent and an apartment along with Vinny's close friend Mack.

Vinny was a tall man with a bald head and brown skin and a very stern but handsome face and a strong athletic body while Mack was just as tall as Vinny,standing 6'3 with thick muscle,bulging pecks,wide shoulders and a strong jawline and square shaped face and dark box shaped haircut,his skin darker than Vinny's,a very dark smooth chocolate brown color that was radiant,and just a tiny shade darker than Jabar's,his face intimidating and stern,but extremely handsome,his eyelashes thick,his age 32 years.

Mack and Vinny were very close,they had met women together,drank together,and even shared their deepest inner secrets with each other,they were more like brothers than friends,tho nothing could rival the relationship Vinny had with Jabar,Jabar being close to a son to him.

Chapter 1

It was a friday night and both Vinny and Mack were sitting in the living area discussing adult and mature in nature topics while they sat back on the sofa a few feet away from each other,beers in their hands.

Man so you telling me you would really let a nigga suck your dick tho,you for real right now? Vinny spoke to Mack as they both conversed back and forth.Hell yea im for real,i let this dude suck my dick one time behind the trashcan when i had just got out the pen that time,nigga sucked it good too,mack spoke to Vinny as Vinny smirked with humor and shock.

You wild man,you wild dawg,i mean i know some niggas might get down in the pen,but damn,right out the joint tho,Vinny spoke to Mack.Yea,but it's whatever now man,i dont get down with that gay shit no more,i leave that shit to them faggots man,that shit aint cool,i would pop a nigga if he came to me with some gay shit now cuz,Mack spoke seriously to Vinny as Vinny lightly nodded his head in agreeance.

Ay dawg chill on that gay shit cuz,i dont want my nephew hearing that shit man,you know how these little young niggas think everything is hip and cool nowadays,next thing you know he wanna suck dick and be with that faggot shit,Vinny cautioned

Mack silently as he saw Jabar exiting his bedroom into the living area.

Man you know on the real tho i would kill a nigga if they was to ever get at Jabar with that gay shit man,im talking about straight up bust a cap in a nigga man,i known that boy since he was just a little dude,this high,i cant imagine some nigga violating him like that,Vinny spoke in all seriousness to Mack as he detailed Jabar's size when he was little with his hands.

Ay nephew,what's popping tonight man,you trying go out with your unc and play some cards at my homeboy Q house in a minute? Vinny spoke to Jabar smoothly as Jabar headed to the fridge for a bottle of water.

Naw,im good unc,im kind of tired tonight for some reason,im going just chill in my room,Jabar spoke to Vinny.Alright,whatever then,yall some weak niggas,Mack bitch ass dont wanna go either,talking about he chilling tonight,im about to roll my ass out in a minute tho,Vinny spoke to jabar as he rose slowly from the sofa he and Mack sat on.

Ay nephew put me a beer in the fridge before you go to sleep or whatever so when i get back that joint be nice and cold,Vinny spoke to Jabar.Alright,i got you Vinny,i put one in there before i get in the shower tonight,Jabar spoke to Vinny.

Alright,that's what's up,i see yall niggas later,im out,Vinny then placed on his coat and grabbed his keys off of the dining room table as he headed out the front door,placing on the bottom lock as he shut the door behind him.

I guess it's just us two niggas here then man,your unc then rolled out on us dawg,shit,im kind of tired too,Mack spoke to Jabar smoothly as he laid himself across the sofa in a manly posture while his eyes then began to watch the television set.

True,but i might be out a little later man,im about to text my friend Blake right fast and hop in the shower,Jabar spoke to Mack as he placed a beer in the fridge freezer for Vinny as he said he would,and then turning to head into his bedroom.

The hours passed,and soon Jabar was showering himself in his own bathroom in his bedroom as Vinny had woken up after a short nap and began to shower in the other room as well,both their naked bodies standing under hot raining showerheads as they soaped themselves under seperate showerheads in seperate rooms.

Vinny finished with his shower first as he stepped out of the bathtub and then placed a clean short above knee length bright white towel around the strong waist of his strong and thick muscled naked body,a body that would put fear in some people because of it's strength and dark muscled thickness.

Jabar finished with his hot shower next,Jabar placing a clean short above knee length white towel around the waist of his toned and very sculpted body as he stepped his feet into shower shoes and then headed out of his bathroom into his bedroom and then into the living area.

Jabar headed out to the fridge to take out Vinny's beer so that it wouldn't freeze too much,his naked body still standing in the towel around his waist and shower shoes on his feet as Mack watched him unknown to Jabar himself.

Damn man,you scared the fuck outta me man,i didn't even see you right there dude! Jabar spoke to Mack as he heard Mack's fidgeting behind him from afar,his body turning towards Mack's.

My bad man,you got out the shower too huh,i just finished with mine,Mack spoke tensely to Jabar as both he and Jabar stared each other down in only the short white towels around the waists of their toned and muscled bodies tensely and somewhat intimately.

Mack intimately watched the innocent and handsome face of Jabar and then Jabar's supple pecks and smooth exposed abs,and then the long toned smooth legs protruding from out of the short white towel around the naked waist of Jabar's sculpted body,and then Jabar's shower shoes,and then back up again.

Jabar intimately but cautiously watched Mack's body up and down as well,starting with Mack's strong handsome face,and then Mack's wide and strong shoulders and muscled arms,and then Mack's bulging pecks and thick abs,and then Mack's thick strong legs that protruded from his short white above knee length towel as well,and then back up to Mack's smooth dark lips.

Jabar tensely reached for a bottle of water to draw distraction from his nervousness and tenseness as he placed the bottle to his lips slowly,placing the bottle tip in first as Mack seemed to watch him even more heavier with an intimate stare.

Mack bit his lip smoothly as he watched Jabar devour the bottle tip with intense eyes,both Mack and Jabar staring eye to eye intimately and silently,Mack watching every angle and smooth graze Jabar's soft lips made across the bottle tip as his mind wandered off to thoughts of mature nature,his body getting a sudden tingling sensation as his eyes continued to fix on Jabar intensely.

Chapter 2

Dawg stop sucking and drinking on that bottle like that man,i swear when people do shit like that it annoy the fuck outta me,Mack spoke to Jabar with a tense facial expression as Jabar eased the bottle from his lips clueless and innocently.

Dude how is me drinking bothering you? Jabar spoke to Mack with slight humor.Man just stop doing it man,or at least do that shit somewhere else,Mack spoke tensely to Jabar,Mack suddenly finding himself in a somewhat fit of sexual frustration that was both known and unknown to him,and he wanted to stop the discreet cause that was only known to himself quickly as he felt his loins tingling down below underneath his towel.

Jabar placed the rest of his bottle of water into the fridge and then lightly reached for Mack's shoulder just as Mack was about to head off.

Man get the fuck off me man,you know what you be doing dude,i aint stupid,i told you stop doing that shit around me,just like i told you stop walking around here like that man,you know what went down last time! Mack yelled at Jabar as he turned back around to face him,anger on Mack's face,and innocence on Jabar's.

Man why you tripping like that man,you cool,you alright? Jabar spoke softly to Mack as he and Mack stared eye to eye.I told you after that first time me and you got down i didn't wanna be around you in positions like this incase we did something we aint supposed to again,before we end up fucking again,you know i got mad love for you man,you know that,and that's why you be fucking with me man,Mack spoke to Jabar as Jabar listened.

Man i dont do shit on purpose to fuck with you man,get that outta your head,but i got love for you too,Jabar spoke to Mack calmly.Nigga you dont love nobody,stop talking fake shit man,Mack spoke to Jabar.Man i do got love for you,i swear i do,what i gotta lie for? Jabar spoke to Mack with conviction.

Then why is that dude always calling your fucking phone then man,huh,what's up with that? Mack spoke to Jabar with curiosity as his eyes nearly pierced through Jabar's skull with their deep intensity.Who you talking about,you talking about Blake tho? Jabar spoke to Mack with confusion.

Yea,Blake or Bleak,or Blike,whatever the fuck his name is,Mack spoke to Jabar.Man Blake just my friend,we just cool,aint nothing between us like that,Jabar spoke to Mack with an honest and sincere tone.

Both Mack and Jabar stared eye to eye as they stood face to face silently,Mack's previous anger starting to subside as he watched Jabar's smooth handsome face.Mack then eased his lips over to Jabar's lips as he let them meet in a silent smooch of their lips softly.

Come here for a second man,Mack guided Jabar into the center of the living area as he began to kiss Jabar again,this time more passionately and deeply.Both Jabar and Mack stood lip to lip and chest to chest and towel to towel and knee to knee as they continued to kiss,Mack then guiding Jabar to his knees near the crotch area of his towel.

Jabar slipped Mack's hardening thick penis into his mouth huge tip first as Mack chucked it into his hand for Jabar's mouth to meet,Jabar's hand pulling off Mack's towel to reveal Mack's full nakedness as he continued to smoothly take Mack's penis into his warm mouth back and forth in wet popping sounds as Mack moaned out softly in pleasure.

Mack continued to push Jabar's head back and forth on his strong dark thick penis as the shaft went back and forth and in and out of Jabar's mouth wet with Jabar's inner mouth as Jabar gagged on it.

Jabar's phone began to ring as it vibrated on the surface of the table lamp near both he and Mack as Mack continued to push his head back and forth onto it harshly in pleasure as he pushed his exposed crotch forward into Jabar's face fastly as if he was making love to Jabar's mouth.

Mack quickly slowed down his stroking rhythm inside Jabar's mouth as he quickly pulled his throbbing penis out of Jabar's mouth and then began to slap it along Jabar's face heavily as it swung back in forth in stiff slinky movements.

Mack then pulled Jabar's towel from his waist as it dropped to the floor below them softly from Jabar's naked body,Mack then forcefully bending Jabar over the sofa as he placed his face inbetween Jabar's naked buttocks,his wet lips giving Jabar's buttocks soft kisses all over and then his lubricated penis penetrating deeply and smoothly inside of Jabar's fleshly walls from the back as he eased himself in further,his own buttocks flexing a bit as his exposed crotch pressed tightly onto Jabar's exposed buttocks.

Mack then began to thrust himself deeply back and forth into Jabar smoothly as he arched Jabar's back a bit further,Jabar feeling Mack's huge warm strong hand on the naked flesh of his back and caressing his naked buttocks from time to time during the strokes of pleasure,Jabar whimpering out as Mack pleasured him from the inside,Mack breathing heavily down Jabar's neck as he continued to pound him from behind,Jabar's fingers shakingly gripping onto Mack's own buttocks as they both moaned and groaned in the heat of sexual pleasure.

What the fuck dawg,i cant be seeing this right now,i fucking cant?! Vinny entered the house with his keys as a bag of soda swung from his other hand,Vinny catching both Jabar and

Mack in their provocative encounter with his very own shocked eyes,eyes that held anger behind them as well,eyes that saw a naked Mack sexually pounding away hardly into a naked Jabar as he laid bent over the sofa looking tiny in comparison to Mack,his rear lifted slightly to the air.

Mack and Jabar quickly disconnected from each other as they began to back away slightly from Vinny in fear and nervousness of being caught.

Chapter 3

Ay Vinny dawg,what's good man,i thought you was playing cards man,Mack slightly stuttered to Vinny out of nervousness as he held and covered his still erected penis with his hand as the rest of his naked body was exposed.

My nephew tho dawg,huh man,huh nigga,you foul like that Mack,huh man?! Vinny spoke angrily but calmly to Mack as he began to take off his coat as if he were preparing for a fight.

Jabar i know you aint with that shit man,tell that nigga you aint with that gay shit,tell him Jabar,i know you aint with that shit,that nigga then gave you something,that nigga give you pills or weed man?! Vinny spoke to Jabar as his voice began to crack into a hoarse sound with building anger.

Uncle Vinny calm down man,alright,let us explain,Jabar spoke timidly to Vinny as Vinny's chest swelled out in rising anger and hurt.Naw,i dont wanna hear shit right now man,save that shit Jabar,im going talk with you later man,i know this aint you,i know you dont get down like that,that nigga then turned you out man,but im about to bust a nigga up right now in the meantime! Vinny spoke to Jabar as he positioned himself in a fighting stance.

Man im not fighting you Vinny,you been my homeboy for 5 years man,look man im sorry,let's squash this shit dude,me and Jabar was just fucking around man,it aint that deep,Mack pleaded to Vinny as Vinny's anger flared even more.

Yall was just fucking around,nigga you was fucking the little dude,had him bent over the couch like he was your bitch,that's a boy,i didn't even know you still got down like that cuz,fuck all that,put up your motherfucking dukes dawg! Vinny angrily shouted at Mack as Mack lightly snickered humorously in response.

Nigga so you think something funny about this shit man?! Vinny yelled to Mack.Naw,you know i dont,im laughing because you tripping right now man,we been boys for too long for me to fight you,Mack spoke to Vinny as he picked up his towel from off the floor to place it back around the waist of his naked body as both he and Vinny stared eye to eye intensely.

Jabar placed his towel back around the waist of his naked body as well,his face innocently and fearfully staring at Vinny.

Man Jabar just tell your unc we got love for each other man,so he wont think im just fucking with your head like some bitch i would on the street,Mack spoke to Jabar as he turned slightly to him,their eyes meeting.

Vinny look dude,i love him alright,Mack spoke to Vinny with seriousness and conviction as he then kissed Jabar passionately on the lips in front of Vinny,causing Vinny's anger to reach it's peak.

Nigga what the fuck you mean yall got love for each other,nigga that's my nephew,he dont look at you like that cuz,stop trying force that gay shit on him dawg,you going stop fucking playing with me! Vinny headed toward Mack with his fist balled angrily to have a physical altercation with him,his face flushed and nearly red with anger,his eyes almost having temporary insanity in them.

Faggot ass nigga man,you wanna go up in niggas nephews dawg,alright! Vinny began to wrestle around with Mack on the floor as they both strongly wrestled each other equally as Jabar watched in fear and regret.

Jabar tried to break Vinny and Mack's fight up,but got punched by accident,Jabar's punch to his face stopping the fight finally as both Vinny and Mack saw Jabar holding his jaw.

Man im sorry Jabar,alright,im sorry man,you should've just let me and your unc fight for minute,we would've got it outta our system,that's mad foul you got hit man,Mack spoke to Jabar apologetically as both he and Vinny stood to their feet.My nephew can take a hit,he aint no soft ass little nigga,Vinny spoke out in order to ease the tension from Jabar being hit.

Let me see man,Mack uncovered Jabar's face from his hand with his own strong hand to see if Jabar was bruised as Vinny flinched discreetly in anger just at the thought and sight of Mack touching Jabar.

You aint bleeding or nothing,you good man,my bad,Mack spoke to Jabar as he examined Jabar's face thoroughly.

All this shit happened because you wanted some ass nigga,you aint no real homeboy dawg,Vinny spoke to Mack,breaking the brief silence that was in the room.You know what man,yep,im going own up to it,me and Jabar was making love before you came in and i was about to get a good ass nut too,Mack spoke proudly and arrogantly to Vinny as Vinny sucked his teeth in an angry response.

Man im going outside to clear my head for minute,if i stay in this joint right now im going fuck somebody up man,i aint trying catch a case! Vinny stormed out of the apartment,slamming the door behind him,leaving Jabar and Mack alone to stare at each other guiltily in quietness.

Two months passed,and soon Vinny was starting to come to terms with the idea that Jabar and Mack were indeed in love,tho he still had trouble adjusting to it completely,Jabar and Mack keeping a low profile on their romance whenever Vinny was around.Tho when Vinny was gone they went all out hard and heavy.

The end

Tale # 2:The laundromat DUDES

By:Anthony Hawkins

Copyright ©2014 by Anthony Hawkins

Cover Art By Anthony Hawkins

Dedicated to the gay and lesbian community.

Prologue

Markeith was 19 years old,and lived with his mother Sharon,they lived in a huge apartment located in a place called denwood springs,the type of apartment you read about and seen in magazines,Each apartment building in denwood springs was included with a laundromat,consisting of washers and dryers,tho the apartments of denwood springs wasn't that bad a place to live in it's neighborhood was a terrible place to live,having ghetto

and sometimes violent
hoodlums,druggies and drunks that
roamed the apartment buildings
every now and then,some leaving
liquor bottles and small tips of
marijuana on the apartment buildings
staircases,even used powdery
substances and used drug needles.

Markeith was the quiet but deadly
type,tho he was quiet,he would
quickly and thoroughly correct
someone if they did him wrong,him
or his family,which was his mother
Sharon and his older cousins Latasha

and Jermaine that lived just a block away from him.

Latasha was Markeith's fast talking and straight to the point cousin,and Jermaine was his shoot first and ask questions later cousin,tho he had respect and a soft spot for family,especially Markeith,his little cousin.Markeith's mother Sharon was the quiet type like Markeith,and would give you the shirt off her back if you needed it,but was quick tempered when it came to her sons safety,her child,which was

Markeith,she was very protective of him.

Markeith was the quiet and currently the only gay one in his family,at least the only one that was out.Markeith was an attractive young man,brown skin,a toned body,and girls and guys lusted for him,tho he only liked guys in that way.

Chapter 1

It was a friday night,and Markeith almost always did his laundry on Friday nights,knowing he would normally have the laundromat to himself,most of his neighbors out clubbing or attending house parties,giving him time to wash his clothing without intrusion or distraction.Markeith had worn most of his clothes the past week and the present week,so he had nothing clean to put on.

Markeith being the hygenic type,he always took a long hot shower before he went washing,therefore he wouldn't enter his clean clothes with a filthy body,and that way he could also include the clothing that he wore and peeled off before his shower into the laundry bag with the rest of his unclean clothes.

Markeith took a hot shower and then placed a short white towel around the waist of his naked body,slipping his feet into a pair of flip flops as he exited the front door of the apartment with his laundry bag in one hand and his keys and mp3 player in the other.Markeith placed the bottom lock on the front door before heading downstairs to the laundry room,his keys rattling with each step he took.

Markeith hovered his laundry bag above the washer machine,letting his dirty clothes fall into the washer,and then placing the bag on the tall bench connected to the wall,pouring a container of detergent into the washer with his clothes,and then pressing the on button as he shut the washer,the slamming sound of the washer being shut echoing through the hallow and silent laundry room,Only Markeith occupying the room.Markeith then sat himself down on the bench as he folded his legs slightly,jamming to his mp3's playlist,his head slightly bobbing as he watched the clothes in the washer machine twirl around in soapy water,his earphones hanging from his ears.

You using the laundry room cuz? A deep but smooth voice spoke to Markeith,interrupting his jamming session,startling him,and causing him slight embarrassment.Oh naw,one of the washers is free,Markeith said to the young guy that stood at the laundry room door,his eyes on Markeith.Alright,cool,the young man spoke as he entered into the laundry room,a bag of dirty clothes dangling from his hand.Shit man,i got two loads to wash cuz,tonight aint my night,wanted to hangout with my homeboy Dee,but i might as well get this washing shit over with,the young man spoke to Markeith as Markeith snickered in response.

Yea,i feel you,Markeith smiled at the guy as the guy poured his clothes and a bottle of detergent into the washer next to the one Markeith was using.

The guy sat himself down on the bench with Markeith,but not within close contact.What chu listening to dawg? The young guy questioned Markeith smoothly,his head turned Markeith's direction.

Markeith felt slightly nervous,seeing that this attractive guy was actually trying to start a conversation with him,but he wasn't sure if the guy was gay or not,so he kept himself cool and collected,hoping he didn't do or say anything to out himself.I was listening to a old joint by lil Raz,but now im listening to this joint by the Yunn's,it's a slow joint,Markeith said nervously to the Handsome young man sitting just a few meters away from him.The yunn's,nigga you for real dawg? The young man smirked,his eyes on Markeith.Yea,they make some good shit,Markeith said softly,his eyes peeping over to the young man slightly,his face nervous.

Markeith wasn't really afraid of the young man,but found the man attractive,that made him sort of shy around the guy.You quiet nigga,but i bet chu be wilding out when you at home by yourself,the young man smiled at Markeith as Markeith smiled back.

I still cant believe you listen to yunn's,they be making some gay shit,mostly them faggot niggas be liking their shit,the young man spoke to Markeith as Markeith became quiet.Nigga you aint cold,you just sitting there in a towel and shit? The young man said to Markeith.Naw,im cool,i always come out like this when im washing,Markeith explained to the guy,his face still slightly nervous.

Not trying call you a faggot,but you should cut the motherfucking yunn's loose dawg,niggas going start thinking you swing like that dawg,if they hear you bumping that shit,im just trying look out for you homey,no disrespect,the young man explained to Markeith.Markeith paused for a few seconds,his eyes no longer on the guy.Why you get so quiet,oh hell naw,you gay dawg? The guy questioned Markeith very silently,eager to hear Markeith's response,developing a somewhat idea why Markeith became so quiet and touchy on the whole gay subject.

If i said yea,then what man? Markeith said silently and timidly.Shit,that's ya business homey,i aint going try and beat cha ass or nothing,you just dont seem gay dawg,that's all,the guy said with confusion covering his face,thinking all gay men were supposed to be overly flamboyant and dressed like women.I am gay man,my pops wont even fuck with me no more,he hung up in my ear when i called him to wish him a happy birthday,the shit is real,Markeith explained,his sensitive side pushing to the surface as he stared to the shiny floor of the laundry room.

Damn,that's cold man,my bad,my pops dead,but at least yours alive man,keep ya head up homey,im Lorenzo,we cool dawg,even if you wit that gay shit,Lorenzo said,pushing his fist to Markeith's.Thank's man,Markeith said quietly to Lorenzo.

Lorenzo laid himself back further onto the bench,and then gapped his legs,holding tightly onto the crotch area of his denim jeans as he stared back and forth at Markeith,Markeith being clueless to the signals Lorenzo was sending him,too nervous to look Lorenzo's way.You gotta little build on you dude,no homo,Lorenzo said to Markeith,trying his best to get Markeith's attention,now gently slapping his leg against Markieth's,giving Markeith a thin smile as Markeith slowly glanced at him,now realizing what type of message Lorenzo was sending him.

Markeith moved himself a little closer to Lorenzo,and then slowly moved his head towards Lorenzo's crotch as Lorenzo unzipped his jeans,biting down on his lower lip,gently sliding his now erect penis into Markeith's warm mouth,a silent moan escaping his lips as his mushroom shaped tip went in first.Lorenzo wanted to take full advantage of the fact that he and Markeith had the secluded laundry room to themselves.

Lorenzo grabbed the back of Markeith's head,pushing Markeith's head further down onto his erect penis,and then began to move Markeith's head back and forth,causing Markeith to gag just a little as he moaned silently.Shit nigga,Lorenzo moaned out quietly as Markeith continued to swallow him,Markeith's head bouncing up and down on Lorenzo's hard penis.Lorenzo began to moan louder in pleasure,feeling the warmth and wetness of Markeith's mouth tightly surround and massage his well endowed penis,his hands groping

Markeith's naked butt cheeks from under Markeith's towel.Gagging sounds filled the laundry room.

Markeith began using a little hand action with his swallowing technique,stroking Lorenzo's penis back and forth in a deep sensual friction as he continued to devour it,letting Lorenzo's penis brush and glide violently but smoothly across the insides of his mouth,until he felt Lorenzo's penis throbbing intensely,quickly and smoothly sliding it out of his mouth as hot semen shot up from the head of Lorenzo's penis,and then slowly dripping down the shaft as Lorenzo moaned and twitched on the bench,still feeling the pleasure and thrilling shock of the orgasm Markeith gave him,his breathing heavy.

Damn dawg,shit man! Lorenzo moaned,another slow shot of semen squirting from the tip of his penis as Markeith watched in excitement and thrill,licking his lips slightly,satisfied with his hot and sticky handiwork,work that he applied to Lorenzo's hard and throbbing penis.

Shit dawg,you got some wipes or something? Lorenzo murmured to Markeith,not wanting his semen to spill onto his jeans.Naw,i aint got nothing on me man,Markeith chuckled,his eyes on Lorenzo.Dawg i gotta change my pants and underwear and shit man,i be back,Lorenzo spoke silently as he eased himself off the bench,quickly zipping his pants back up and then heading towards the laundry room door.Thank's cuz,Lorenzo said quietly to Markeith before exiting the

laundry room,the door shutting
behind him.

Chapter 2

Markeith in some ways felt like a
cheap male whore,giving oral sex to a
young man he barely knew,and then
hearing the word thank's depart from
the mans lips after the job was
done,but tho Markeith felt cheap,he
also got his own thrills out of it,so
that lessened the cheap feeling he
felt.

Markeith headed over to the washer machine,seeing the washer stop it's spinning,and then placed his hot and wet clothes into one of the dryers,sliding his laundry money card across it,a card that only people who lived in the apartments had access to,and then he started the dryer,sitting down on the bench as his clothes began to spin in the heating dryer.

Lorenzo entered the laundry room again,now wearing a pair of sweat pants,his eyes instantly focusing on Markeith as he entered the room,sitting himself next to Markeith again.You got some good ass dome dawg,i forgot chu gay tho,ya'll niggas like sucking dick,i know how ya'll dudes roll,Lorenzo snickered,his head towards Markeith's stare.Dude all gay dudes dont give head,that shit is a stereotype,it's tops and bottoms,some tops might give head,mainly the verse tops,but most tops dont,and some bottoms dont either,Markeith explained to Lorenzo,a smirk on his face.

And how the hell you talking shit,when i just gave you head nigga,you might as well call yourself gay too dude,Markeith spoke to Lorenzo,still smirking.What the fuck is a top? And nigga you gave me head dawg,i aint the gay one nigga,Lorenzo chuckled in denial,thinking only guys who received were gay,but not the giver,not realizing that if he had any sexual feelings towards another male that he was either gay or bisexual himself.

Dawg you trying see my homeboy? Lorenzo questioned Markeith as

Markeith's face lit with confusion.Huh? Markeith said.My homeboy trying get it in too,you down dawg? Lorenzo spoke to Markeith as Markeith gathered his thoughts quickly,realizing that Lorenzo wanted him to give his homeboy the same thing he gave him,which was oral sex,Lorenzo telling his friend about he and Markeith's encounter,and boasting to him about how Markeith gave better oral sex than any female he had been with.Naw,this aint some shit i do on a regular basis,Markeith explained to Lorenzo as Lorenzo listened.

I get dude to pay you son,Lorenzo said to Markeith as Markeith began to chuckle in response.Are you serious dude? Markeith laughed out.Yea,all jokes aside,i can get my dude to pay you son,if you dont wanna do the shit just to do it,you like dick,shit,Lorenzo said to Markeith,a thin smile on his face.Whatever dude,nigga aint gotta pay me,just bring ya homeboy here,and just hope we dont get fucking caught,Markeith chuckled silently,his eyes on Lorenzo,Markeith feeling that doing Lorenzo's friend would be something new and kinky.Alright dawg,that's what's up,imma get at him now,im about to call him up,Lorenzo spoke as he pulled his cellphone from his pants pocket,pressing speed dail.

Hello?! A deep voice answered Lorenzo's call.Yea dawg,this me,dude said he going do it cuz,come down dawg,Lorenzo said to the man on the phone.Alright,that's what's up,i be down there,the deep voiced man spoke,he and Lorenzo now ending their call.

A tall young handsome man with dreadlocks entered the laundry room minutes later,his skin dark,nearly close to black,his teeth straight and white,his pants sagging,exposing his boxer briefs.This my homeboy i was telling you about,Lorenzo explained to Markeith,letting Markeith know that the man with the dreadlocks was his friend,the friend he wanted Markeith to show a good time.Markeith was tall,but not as tall as Lorenzo or Lorenzo's dreadlock wearing friend.Tho Markeith was a man himself,Markeith felt somewhat intimidated,having two guys in the laundry room at once,feeling as if he was being overpowered.

What's up cuz? Lorenzo's friend nodded at Markeith,no smile on his face,only a let's get down to business look.Markeith waved his hand smoothly at Lorenzo's friend,giving him a greeting with his hand.Lorenzo's friend slowly pulled down his boxers,exposing the thin ebony pubic hair on his crotch,and his huge ebony penis with a plump pink mushroom shaped tip.

What's good dude? Come and do ya thang,Lorenzo's friend spoke silently and seductively to Markeith,his eyes watching Markeith intensely.My homeboy Tavion cool,stop acting shy nigga,Lorenzo said silently to Markeith,wanting Markeith to loosen up,and go over to his dreads wearing friend Tavion.

Markeith headed over to Tavion,and then got to his knees as Tavion towered over him,their eyes making contact.Just suck it dude,you cool,Tavion said silently and softly to Markeith,holding his shirt up with one hand,slightly exposing his abs,while his other hand held onto his erect penis,Tavion wanting and waiting for Markeith's mouth to accompany it as Lorenzo pulled Markeith's towel from off his waist,leaving Markeith's toned body naked and exposed as he groped Markeith's exposed buttocks with lust and expectations.

The end

www.ingramcontent.com/pod-product-compliance
Lightning Source LLC
Chambersburg PA
CBHW020348290526
45785CB00005B/2188